failure project
by yolanda mercy

failure project premiered at Summerhall on 1 August 2024
as part of the Edinburgh Festival Fringe

failure project
by yolanda mercy

Performer	Yolanda Mercy
Co-direction	Joseph Barnes-Phillips Yolanda Mercy
Dramaturgy	Joseph Barnes-Phillips Jules Haworth
Set Design	Yolanda Mercy Joseph Barnes-Phillips
Costume Design	Yolanda Mercy Joseph Barnes-Phillips
Sound recording/design	Mikaiyiri Joseph Barnes-Phillips
Poster Photographer	Richard Haynes
Poster Designer	Yolanda Mercy

Voice-overs are pre-recorded by Yolanda Mercy. With special thanks to Joseph Barnes Phillips, Thais Wizenberg and Michael Magambo (for additional ad-libs/support).

Yolanda Mercy

Yolanda is an award-winning British Nigerian writer, director and performer from London. Her TV writing has been has nominated for BAFTA, WGGB and Broadcast Awards. She also won the Edinburgh TV Festival Debut TV Writer Award. Yolanda originally began creating work within theatre, and has expanded her practice to TV, film and audio. Her theatre work inclues *Quarter Life Crisis* which won the Underbelly Untapped Award and debuted at Edinburgh Fringe 2017. In 2024, Summerhall awarded Yolanda the prestigious Meadows Award for failure project, which debuted with them August 2024.

Some of Yolanda's writing credits include *On The Edge of Me* (Soho Theatre and UK tour); *Quarter Life Crisis* (Underbelly and UK/international tour); *Quarter Life Crisis* (BBC Radio 1xtra); *BBW* (Channel 4); *World of Curls* (BBC Radio 4) and *In Between Two Places* (BBC Radio 4).

Some of Yolanda's acting credits include *On The Edge of Me* (Soho Theatre and UK tour); *Quarter Life Crisis* (Underbelly and UK/international tour); *Quarter Life Crisis* (BBC Radio 1xtra); *BBW* (Channel 4) and *World of Curls* (BBC Radio 4).

Some of her other awards and affiliations include BFI Network x BAFTA crew mentee; Soho Theatre's Soho Six, JMK Mentee with the JMK Trust and Peggy Ramsay/Film4 Playwright Award winner.

Joseph Barnes-Phillips

Joseph Barnes-Phillips is an award-winning multi-disciplinary artist, whose practices in performing, producing, directing, writing, composing, casting and community engagement has pioneered and enriched Black British contemporary theatre for over a decade.

Joseph's Guyanese and Black British heritage has gifted him the privilege of creating unforgettable shows, leaving many audiences members 'feeling seen and heard'.

As a Black man born and raised in south-east (deep south) London, his passion for folklore, storytelling, subculture and world-building has had Joseph's work published through a variety of creative mediums, programming live performance, radio, TV, film, animation and commercials.

His production, *Big Foot*, is a raw and highly passionate stage play that challenges the stereotype of what it means to be a young Black male in modern Britain.

Audiences have said that 'Joseph Barnes-Phillips writes with emotive, close-to-home clarity about longing, fatherhood, and love.'

Big Foot was originally commissioned by Black Theatre Live and had a 2017 tour across the UK. It was published by Aurora Metro Books.

Other writing credits include a HuffingtionPost article *I Created A Theatre Show To Stamp Out The Stereotypes Of A Young Black Man*, *PUP!* commission by Theatre Royal, Bury Saint Edmunds; *Big Smother* commissioned by Oval House and produced by HighRise Theatre, *The Concrete Jungle Book* produced by Arts Depot and HighRise Theatre, *The UK Drill Project* commissioned by the Barbican and winner of the Samuel Beckett Award 2020, play staged 2022, where Joseph was executive director and executive producer; *Penny Lane* commissioned by The Yard Theatre; *Merryville* a co-production with CPT, and supported by Cardboard Citizens, Home Truths Young Company Bursary, developed in partnership with CPT and Jerwood Foundation; *HighRise Podcast*, commissioned by Hunt & Darton's Radio Local.

Director credits include *Aci by the River* at River Stage, produced and commissioned by the National Theatre; Associate Director and Choreographer for DK Flash. Joseph was also Young Company Director at Orange Tree Theatre.

Acting credits include *Black Power Desk* (Bristol Old Vic Actor's Lab), *Huddle* (Unicorn Theatre, winner of the Offies Award for Productions for Young People 0-7 in 2019), *World of Curls* (BBC Radio 4).

Credits as Casting Director include Miraa Mary's *Nobody* (music video) directed by Mahaneela Choudhury; *The Wave: Nike x Patta*, directed by Mahanella Choudhury and Steve McQueen.

Joseph is creating an exciting immersive experience that celebrates the ancestral practice of storytelling and horticulture. *Grounding in Nature* both promotes and cultivates self-development and forces a human being to be 'wholehearted'.

'Wonderfully entertaining, Joseph Barnes-Phillips delivers an important message through his colossal performance. ★★★★' *MyTheatreMates.com* on *Big Foot*

Jules Haworth

Jules is a queer and disabled dramaturg and access support worker with a focus on supporting and developing emerging writers and artists.

As Creative Engagement Associate at Soho Theatre, she co-runs the prestigious Writers' Lab programme, and has run playwriting workshops and talks with Talawa Theatre, Graeae, Rich Mix, LGBTQ+ Arts, Sour Lemons, Gendered Intelligence, Traverse Theatre, Live Theatre, National Youth Theatre, Somerset House and in schools and colleges across London.

As a dramaturg, Jules has worked on award-winning plays including *Brute* by Izzy Tennyson (Underbelly); *Muscovado* by Matilda Ibini (Theatre503 and tour); *Villain* by Martin Murphy (Underbelly, Kings Head Theatre); *On the Edge of Me* by Yolanda Mercy (Soho Theatre and UK tour); *Quarter Life Crisis* by Yolanda Mercy (Soho Theatre and international tour), *Wonderboy* by Ross Willis (Bristol Old Vic); *Dust* by Milly Thomas (Soho Theatre, Trafalgar Studios); *Algorithms* by Sadie Clark (Pleasance, Soho Theatre, Park Theatre) and *Little Miss Burden* by Matilda Ibini (Bunker Theatre).

Jules also co-runs the networking group Theatre Queers and is a board member for Milk Presents. Her play *Pigeon Steps* was longlisted for the Adrian Pagan Award 2014.

Mikaiyiri

Mikaiyiri [pronounced mikai-yi-lee] is a soulful singer-songwriter, multi-instrumentalist and producer. He merges alternative, r&b, folk, and rap influences into melodic, raw and heartfelt song. Born and raised in East London, he grew up listening to an eclectic mix of music which has given him a particular taste for chords and harmonies.

He collaborated with David Senoga and Bambino (Isaac Mugerwa) to create music for the *failure project*.

failure project

Yolanda Mercy

This is for us. 'We gon' be alright'

Writer's Note

This is a play written for writer-performers. Those multi-hyphenates who want to get on stage and share a story that means something to them, and hopefully resonates with an audience. So make this play your own. The words sound like how you'd actually speak, with a little bit of poeticness to it. That's intentional. This play is meant to feel real, 'cause I can't pretend these things don't happen and won't still happen. I've written this to be honest, so don't change my words – I've spent SO much time working on this script but I give you creative licence to finesse it. Make it your own. Embody it, and make it something that you love performing (as much as I do).

I love a good '…' during sections of dialogue, which means find space to get into the character, play, make your audience laugh (or cry) use this play as a platform to showcase you… 'cause I think you're pretty awesome for wanting to perform *failure project*.

Yolanda Mercy
July 2024

Thank-yous

Obvs my mum, sis, dad… My family and friends for supporting me. Joseph Barnes-Phillips and Jules Haworth for collaborating with me. Summerhall for debuting the play. Tom Forster for believing in me. Waitrose for the sponsorship. Nick Hern Books team for bringing me into the NHB family. And to you for picking up this playtext.

Characters

ADE, *early thirties*
LEANNE, *early thirties*
MUM, *mid-fifties*
DAD, *late fifties*
JESSICA, *late twenties*
TOBI (*voice-over*), *early thirties*
EMILY, *early thirties*
STRANGER (*voice-over*), *early thirties*
LU, *mid-twenties*
DENISE, *mid-twenties*
OTHER BLACK GIRL, *mid-thirties*
TING, *mid-thirties*
LOTTIE (*voice-over*), *early thirties*
NURSE (*voice-over*), *mid-fifties*
COMMENTS (*voice-over*), *ageless*
SIRI (*voice-over*), *thirties*

Rules of the Script

An ellipsis (…) denotes a moment for the actor to play with (see Writer's Note above for more info, hun).

Gaps between the lines are to replace *Beat*. Meaning, allow yourself to find moments to let the words land.

Original Set Information

A row of stemmed roses lay on the stage floor.

This text went to press before the end of rehearsals and so may differ slightly from the play as performed.

Pre-Show

The preshow is upbeat. At the three-minute call there's a voice-over from ADE *and* SIRI.

ADE	Hey friend, it's me Ade Adeyomi… I know you've just arrived at the theatre, you're all sweaty, need to go for a pee, or you're tryna get a quick bevvy… or let's be real – you're checking to see if the boy you fancy is watching your Insta stories? Yeah, I know. Even though he hasn't responded to your messages for what three days???… it's like BITCH you know I can see you watching my stories… you know that right?? Right?!!!! Okay!… Just me?!
	I can hear the silence… It's real loud. Like REAL REAL LOUD. Yikes… that was a MAJOR overshare on my part, I'm gonna bring this ish up when I eventually go to therapy or I'll ask Siri…
SIRI	hey girl heyyyyy, what's good?
ADE	what does it mean if a guy watches your stories but doesn't respond to your text?
SIRI	sis, will you ever get tired of pouring out your personal life in these metaphorical theatrical streets?
ADE	Siri, nobody wants to hear that. Read the room… Literally!!!
SIRI	ohhhh we're at one of your shows?
ADE	yep! You've made it into another one of my shows

SIRI – are you gonna trade me in for – (*Whispers.*) Alexa?!

ADE girl, I wouldn't do that, you know this hoe is loyal… but we're gonna have to talk about this later. 'Cause I'm feeling a lil judged by you. You usually have my back when it comes to all things boys, symptoms diagnosis and language translation

SIRI – my bad, baby girl, you know I didn't mean it like that… I've been going through a lot of changes. These updates be messing with me and whatnot

ADE mmhmmm, if you say so. We'll talk about this later.

SIRI *whispers in the background.*

SIRI sorry

ADE Anyway. Party people… and I mean YOU, you who have come to see the show, please take your seat, they're comfortable I promise. We're about to beginnnnnnnnn

Stage lights on.

Scene One

Upbeat music shifts.

ADE (*aside*) …at the beginning of every show I like to welcome the audience in
make them feel like this is their home for the next forty-five, fifty or sixty minutes… depending on my script commission.

I know I shouldn't say this but theatre want a full-length script on a half-length budget.

I get logically why shows have to be sixty minutes plus, 'cause ticket prices can't be less than £15 or the theatre wouldn't make enough money.

The box-office team wouldn't get paid

so there'd be no ushers
              no tech crew
              no show

just an empty theatre space or black box.

Silence.

But there'd still be actors
there'd be storytellers making shows in their bedrooms
      at home
           on the Tube.
Working hours longer than is legal to make enough money to rent a space, to share their work…
    their art
         even if it isn't paid
                they do it 'cause it's a drug…
                      an addiction to
being heard in a world filled with perfectly curated lives…
'cause no one actually wants to know how you feel unless you're in a theatre
or writing a novel
                which isn't about you…

but everyone low-key questions if it's about you

the characters sound like you…
                and your friends…

So it's kinda like
'is it art imitating life'
>or just
>>'a memoir on stage'…
>You know

Pause.

(*aside*) they both look at me… Unsure of what to make of what I've said… 'Cause I was talking way too fast. I know I was… and I jumped through way too many points for them to actually know what I'm talking about…
The producer – Jessica – routinely takes a sip of her coffee… or should I say the empty cup that once had coffee but is now just remnants of bubbles and backwash 'cause I'm pretty sure I've seen her, and her assistant Lu, share from the same espresso cup…
>and I'm not cup-shaming
but it's an espresso cup… there's barely enough caffeine for one.

JESSICA I like where you're going with this Ade… It's slay! The embodiment of Siri as a real person that… That is genius –

ADE (*aside*) wait did she just say I'm genius?

JESSICA – but. I'm struggling to get a sense of *you*… or the community you represent. how does it feed into the opening of *Day Girl*? It needs to announce the show and your voice. I'm eager to get a sense of you, without *you* actually being there. We need to feel more of Ade 'the writer's' presence through the words, but still leave enough space for Denise, or any actor, to find themselves in it… It's just missing something… An authenticity or grounding of sorts to make it London yet still universal. But

	what do I know, I went to international school. Lu, what are your thoughts?
ADE	(*aside*) she turns to look at her assistant Lu, who assisted her in finishing off her espresso to confirm her thoughts. Her contradictory thoughts that she's disguised as questions, but are definitely a statement. Lu looks down before clearing her throat
LU	I mean I'm not from London either. Who is?
ADE	(*aside*) I am... Hey, I was born in St Thomas' Hospital... representing Londonnnnnn. South London... but okay... Lu continues
LU	I have to agree with Jess's point.
JESSICA	Thank you, Lu. Ade, you are a brilliant writer, performer, multi-hyphenate... we love what you've penned for *Day Girl*... how nuanced it is about the UK public schooling system, and your struggles of being the working class scholarship kid in a predominately... JESSICA *pauses trying to find the right word to say. She wants to say 'white' and 'middle' class...* Eurocentric school. Your words are honest, warm and hilarious
LU	It's funny... you... the script gets me giggling... every time
JESSICA	– Ade, I believe there is more you can get from the script. And the closer we get to casting announcements, and Susie executing her direction, and refining the show with Denise. We need to make it easier for them. I mean it's only a one-person play, it's extremely exposing

ADE (*aside*) They look at me, and wait for my response. I nod diligently. Even though there is a lot I want to say but I don't... It's not worth it

JESSICA – I'm thrilled you agree. Let us know how you get on. Apologise Susie couldn't be here, you know how it is with rehearsals. Denise needs a lot of alone time with her.

ADE yeah I understand.

JESSICA of course you do, you're an actor. Slay.

ADE they routinely place their pens into the spines of their Moleskines, which is the universal sign for 'this meeting is over'... I gather my things and leave the theatre space. The place that in 4 short weeks will be filled with an audience ready to see my second play, *Day Girl*.

They commissioned the play... the slightly fictionalised story of my experience as a day girl at an elite private school.
Mum was determined I'd get into that school, with a scholarship. And I did.

A sign of triumph to her, was my label of shame to them. They'd always point at me in the classroom, corridor, canteen – or wherever I was, there was NO escaping the

'What's gwaning scholarship kid?'...

Actually that's tame, they'd say

'I'm glad my parents donated to Comic Relief. Now we can help poor African kids like you'...

like I said I was born in St Thomas' Hospital, and even if I was born in Africa it doesn't

mean I'm poor... we have billionaires in
Africa.

                              But they didn't care.

To them I was black
        so I'm poor.

I told the producers, Jessica and Lu, about my
experience at school
they nodded
they sympathised
and even cried

They asked me how quickly I could get it on
to a page.

Truth is I had a lot of work on... work I wasn't
paid for... but it's still work...
But this
    this was a paid opportunity to get my
work on a stage that I have never been on
before.

Within a month I delivered *Day Girl*
Within 2 months I got paid
Within 3 months they programmed it with
hardly any changes.
Or so I thought.
Within 4 months they hired Susie the director
Within 5 months Susie felt it would be better
to separate my roles...
Within 6 months I was no longer the Actor...
Writer for this show. I was just the writer.
With threads
        upon threads
                of notes
                        upon notes

JESSICA   (*voice-over*) We love the script. But we have some *slight* tweaks...

ADE *tries to speak but is talked over.*

>   We think it would be a good idea to change
>   the main character, since you're not in the
>   show any more...
>
> ADE *tries to speak but is talked over.*
>
>   At its core this is a Londoner's, working-
>   class story. A story about someone trying
>   to navigate the UK class system... it's a
>   universal story that anyone can relate to. Let's
>   explore this in casting...

ADE So they did.
They hired a more 'relatable actor'
An influencer who looked nothing like me
But the weight of her following could sell out
a 4-week run in a *slightly* off-West End venue.
Even though she's never acted before
                                her following
had enough influence to bring in the
demographic that *they*'d historically alienated.
My agent, Lottie, tried to reassure me by
moving my attention from something I've
already written, and focus on what I'm doing
next.

And I know she's right.
         I've 'got so much work'...
                      Even if it's unpaid...

but when I pour my words on to a page and
expect to see myself or the story I intended to
tell, I can't hide the fact that it hurts. Even just
a little bit.

Has that ever happened to you?

Have you ever dreamed of something just
to be told by someone that we'll buy your
dreams but we'll erase you out of it.

I think all of this bittersweetly as I journey

down the crimson corridors of the theatre, and
head to the green
       exit.

ADE *stops. Smiles. Waves* (*a little*).

On my way out I spot Denise, she beckons me
into the rehearsal room...
I crack open the door and Susie's face reads
'bitch we don't want you here'
but Denise has the influence
       the final say.

I sit down next to Susie and smile, then turn
back to Denise who launches into the scene

DENISE   Nah man, u lots r pagans for dat, I'm not sum
nxt souf London chick dat u preppy kids can
play wiv still ya nah.

DENISE *kisses her teeth.*

ADE*'s facial expression is HARD to read.*

ADE   (*aside*) I watch Denise recite words upon
words back to me
back to me in a blaccent with a slight twinge
of an MLE accent
vowels that she's revelling in
consonants that she's playing with
Finding her rhythm in
       that I know I definitely did *not* write

DENISE   nah man bun u lots I'm leavin dis skool 4 real.

ADE*'s phone rings. It's kinda obnoxious. She
cancels the call.*

ADE   Sorry it's my mum.

ADE *texts her mum.*

(*aside*) I quickly text my mum

'IM AT WORK, CALL U LATER'

                              In caps.

                    I know I shouldn't.
                              Not in caps.
                                        That's disrespectful.

                    I follow it up with a love heart emoji.

                    Before looking back at Denise who
                    continues…

                    ADE *puts her phone away.*

DENISE   So what did you think Ade? Some of the
                    words aren't the same as your script. I didn't
                    vibe with them too tuff. I've heard TV actors
                    change up the words all the time and writers
                    are cool with that. So I thought theatre would
                    be the same. Collaborative and whatnot…

ADE   Collaborative. Yeah. (*aside*) I hate it… I really
                    fucking hate it.

                    As always I wonna say more.
                    But I don't.
                    I can't.

                    And judging by Susie's expression I've
                    definitely overstayed my welcome.

                    For the second time this afternoon. I gather
                    my things. Say my goodbyes and finally leave
                    the theatre…
                    Kinda

                    ADE *breaths in the fresh air outside.*

                    It's nice to be in the real world again

                    even just for a minute.

                    I jump onto the Northern Line from Tottenham
                    Court Road and head to another theatre, eager
                    to make it there before rush hour…

                    Sounds of the Tube.

Scene Two

Sounds of the Tube morph into sounds of the street outside of the theatre.

ADE even though I'm at the theatre an hour earlier than is needed…
I prefer it…
It's like an act of rebellion, a peaceful protest against the stereotype that black people are always late.

Now I'd like to say that I've always been part of the early crew, but as a child raised in the church of BPT
     Black people time. It took some getting used to.
Some prayer and deliverance
And in my deliverance I found out that being on time is basically being late.
From that point on I decided that I'd always be   an hour early for everything…
Birthdays
     Funerals
          And 'Netflix and chill'…

I need some time to actually chill before 'Netflix'…

I think all of this as I find my way to my seat.
Eager for the play to begin.
A play called *Show 2*…
A surprise show
     that will be revealed to 'us' the audience when the show begins.

I don't usually like surprises
I don't usually visit this theatre
but for the first time in a long time they've advertised for an associate playwright role…

I've never been associated to anything
                              or anyone...

So I thought I'd apply...

I take my time to observe the audience as they mill into the unfamiliar auditorium.
I take my seat and I wait
I know I'm early
It's only 7.15
But I like the wait
The peace

ADE *looks to the left and notices someone staring at her.*

You know that feeling
        that feeling that you get when you know someone is staring at you...
No.
    Glaring at you
               that's happening to me right now.
I take my phone out and pretend to look at something...
        anything...
I scroll Instagram then I feel someone tap
                      tapping on
my shoulder.
The couple that were glaring at me from the end of the row are now next to me...
                Next to me and
accompanied by an usher in a bright red shirt who is towering over where I'm sat.

USHER   Excuse me, can I see your ticket?

ADE   (*aside*) being asked to see my ticket is giving me major ticket inspector PTSD. I don't know what it is but when a ticket inspector asks to see my ticket I get all nervous
        and flustered
                and I start sweating
                        A LOT

And my words get all jumbly
And mixed up
And I act like I don't have a ticket...
      even though I know I do...
        I definitely do.
Well that's happening to me right now
In this theatre that I'm not associated with

But I would like to be.

So I keep fumbling around my bag, looking for my ticket

And I can feel the heat from the couple shooting daggers my way.
I find my ticket
finally
  and present it to the usher. She glances at it and then the couple's.

USHER   it seems you both have the same seats.

ADE   She's talking at me
It's blatantly obvious she's looking in my direction.
But doesn't actually say it to me.
Like so many people in my life
Who act like I'm not really there
      even though I am.
She continues with

USHER   maybe you're meant to be in the upper circle not the stalls

ADE   (*aside*) I get all flustered again
especially 'cause two people have now sat on the other side of me, and the pre-show call rattles
  in
the distance

Pre-show call: 'Ladies and gentlemen, please take your seats, this evening's performance will begin in five minutes. Please take your seats.'

Did I make a mistake? I'm pretty sure I
booked the stalls, but like I said I haven't
been to this theatre in ages, I could of made a
mistake.

So I pick up my bag and coat, and then I see
it...
I tell her what I have seen
She checks to see what I have seen
                        It's there
My ticket is for today and theirs was for
yesterday.
The usher leans forward
They lean forward...
and inspect to see if I was wrong...
                        but I wasn't.
They flush red. The usher places the ticket
back into my hand and sort of smiles at my
direction... but weirdly still *not* looking at
me... before walking off with the couple.
They leave me behind without an apology and
an embarrassment that shouldn't belong to
me.
But it does
There is a shame that rests on my shoulders.
Even the people next to me notice it.
They turn their backs to me...

So I shrink
I wrap my arms tightly around my body.
Careful not to take up too much space.
Space in places that don't always welcome
bodies like mine.
I sink into my seat for the whole two hours...
Two and half hours of a mystery text, with no
interval
     No chance for your girl to escape the
theatre, run away from another traumatising
show about slavery.

ADE *exhales heavily.*

The lights go out. The audience stand, they cry.
And I don't know what to do... I feel heavier than when I came in. I look to my left and I see another black girl, whose face reads with the same expression as mine.
She does the nod.
I nod back...
The universal signal of our mutual recognition and respect.

As soon as the show's done, I swiftly leave.
She... The other black girl catches up with me.

We talk, vibe, and even laugh through the pain...
Some people call that 'black girl magic'... I like to call it 'black girl strength'...
Our ability to keep going even when we feel like we can't...
A guy taps us on the shoulder.
Tells us we were amazing in the show.
We both want to say something
                             anything
But he walks away before we can.
We both look at each other with an expression that reads 'let's talk about that later'.
We both laugh.
It's nice to laugh
To feel a moment of black girl joy amidst a whole lot of mess.
She then looks at me and we pick up from where we left off.
She tells me that she's a writer... I tell her I am also, she says

OTHER BLACK GIRL   Sis, I've heard about you and your show. It's a big deal, girl... everyone knows about it. It's hard for us to get a show on in a

venue like that. You're paving the way for us.
Keep being booked and busy

ADE I smile.
If only she knew the truth of what booked,
busy and so-called blessed looked like.
My mind has been jumping between
Day Girl edits
Developing ideas
General meetings
Reading novels
Pitching for novels
Pitching my ideas
        Reworking my ideas
        Reworking
        Working
        Working
        Work
        Work

Edits
    Edits
        Final edit
        Final draft
            done

And don't forget

Never forget to call Mum back...

                She'll think
you're dead, otherwise.

I think all of this as we eventually say our
goodbyes and I head on the Tube, and journey
down south... Back to ends...

Four Tube stops later I finally submerge from
the station.

I pick up the phone and I buzz Tobi...

Tobi's my best friend who I've known since I
was a teenager

The only person that makes this world a better place

ADE *picks up the phone and calls* TOBI.

TOBI You've reached the voicemail for Tobi Oludeji. You know what to do.

ADE Hey Tobi, it's me... Why did I say that, you know it's me...

ADE (*on voicemail*) Chileee today was mad. It was giving team too much. I had a whole fight without having to fight a bitch in the theatre, 'cause you know I wouldn't do that... that's le ghetto. I'm still trying out putting 'le' in front of everything. Something about using a French word makes everything sound more bougie... Le ghetto... Also, on a lighter note, I can't say 'slay' any more, one of my work colleagues has now started using it all the time in the wrong context and it's just not giving. I'm gonna look for a new word. Anyway. Miss you

ADE *hangs up the phone, exhales. Touches her heart...*

What do you do when you have pain?

I mean we all touch it and try to relieve it somehow.
If I'm honest, a lot of us tend to ignore it.
We don't want it to hold us back.
We don't have the time.

Nobody does.

I think all of this... and kinda say it out loud as he looks at me.

Surrounded by all of the stuff in my flat, and it almost looks like he's home.
But he's not.

It's not his.
It's mine.
It's my flat.
But he's my 'ting'?!
    my Marcus.
    my 'Situationship'.

A situationship is a relationship that pendulums between not being together, but acting like we are
  even though we know we aren't
                    we definitely aren't
it's been discussed
it's cool
I'm cool
Totally cool.
It's been four months and twenty-two days
Who cares.
Not me.
I'm fine.

Cool.
It's cool.

He's 'figuring things out' and I'm busy with…
                      You've seen.
It works for both of us
    living in the see-saw of uncertainty.
Certain that we're both enjoying each other's company.

Marcus sits on the edge of my bed. Halfway between dressed and showing off his arm tatts that make me forget what day of the week it is… 'cause it's not important.
I mean it is important
But when I'm with him who gives a fuck about time

ADE *looks at him*.

Wonna stay over? You haven't stayed in ages

TING	Babe, I want to but I can't. Work is a bit mad. My boss is leaving and it's added more to my workload and… You know what that's like… Actually what am I saying. You're a writer. You're basically a socialite
ADE	How am I a socialite?
TING	You sit around all day masturbating, going to pilates or yoga then hitting up fancy drinks and occasionally writing. Socialite.
ADE	I don't masturbate all day… Any more… I read an article in *Women's Health* that said you could reduce your pleasure sensation if you do
TING	Don't believe everything you read online. You should know that as a writer… Or should I say 'part timer'
ADE	Marcus I'm not a part-timer!
TING	When was the last time you wrote something new?
ADE	I wrote *Day Girl*. That's new and I'm working on pitches to share with production companies
TING	What? Those slide shows I see you creating with bare pictures?
ADE	They're not *just* pictures. They're perfectly curated photos that make up a story. A narrative
TING	Rigggght. An adult picture book. Which isn't something that you're writing… and you're doing for free?! Explain to me how you're not a socialite. You technically don't work
ADE	(*aside*) I want to explain to him, like I have so many times before, about the process of my job. But he doesn't get it

	He can't comprehend the idea of spending hours 'working up an idea' to share with someone, who may or may not like it… And not getting paid for it. 'cause outside of this industry people don't usually work for free
TING	Anyway babes. Some of us have to make some money. You should go see your doctor about your… pain. You've got the time.
ADE	(*aside*) He kisses me on the forehead and leaves. Leaves me empty like so many times he has before.

Silence.

by the way, I don't masturbate every day… It's more like every other day.

A buzzing sound morphs into the sound of Skype.

(*aside*) I haven't used Skype in ages. The only reason why I'm on here at 9 a.m., on a Tuesday is 'cause of her, Emily.
Emily's the development manager at a big production company
She gives me a breakdown of their company
Their merger
And what they've been working on…
Judging from her tone, I can't tell if she's happy about this
    or not.
British people are the master of subtext.
Emily stops weaving the past and present history of her company, and leaves space for me to fill in mine. My story and the idea I want to share with her.

I open my 'adult picture book' and tell her about one of my ideas

ADE *clears her throat*.

The idea is about a black woman called Dami who is a scientist at a competitive UK space agency. Dami is driven, passionate and works by the book, however she discovers that her workplace's practices aren't ethical and it makes her question: does she stand up for what she believes in, or say nothing to progress in her career.

ADE *looks down*.

(*aside*) I'm really passionate about this idea. I love it. I really fucking love it. The chance to explore science and have a black female lead. This is where ya girl aka me wants to be at.

But judging from Emily's dwindling expression. I can tell she's not feeling this idea.

ADE *looks down*.

but then the craziest thing happens to her. Dami, returns to her locker and finds a note that says 'you should go back to your country…'

(*aside*) Emily's facial expression changes, I think she's going to cry.
I can't handle tears over Zoom
Sorry, I mean Skype
It's a natural post-pandemic reflex
Tears = a bitch could get fired
And that bitch is me
                me who is booked, busy and hopefully blessed enough to get that Skype merger coins.

Emily clears her throat and pats a potential tear away from her eye.

EMILY	I can see this now. The struggles and challenges that a character like Dami could face. It has a strong underline of racial tension, and confronts what it means to be Black and British in the UK
ADE	(*aside*) why is when I talk about something traumatic then I'm heard? Like black people don't wonna go space? Like hello *Space Jam*
EMILY	This idea is something that I think I could bring to my bosses. They're always looking for stories like this. We also have a project, that we are looking for a writer on. It's about a boy called JJ. JJ is twelve, from Nigeria but moved to Croydon with his family when he was eight. He struggled to adjust at school because of the language barriers
ADE	(*aside*) by the way we speak English in Nigeria… colonisation was REAL
EMILY	societal differences and his undiagnosed learning difficulties made it challenging for him to navigate the UK schooling system, then he ultimately was excluded, groomed into a gang and was shot dead in a playground.
	ADE *gasps. Shocked. Slightly frozen in fear.*
ADE	(*aside*) I didn't mean to gasp like that so dramatic like that… but I wasn't expecting to hear this. I wasn't expecting to
EMILY	– we had a writer. But they can no longer do it, and we think you'd be a good match. You're Nigerian right?
ADE	umm… I… yes I am
EMILY	perfect. We thought you'd understand this story, and get this culturally accurate. What

>   we can do is send you over a bunch of the
>   materials, there are voicenotes from JJ's
>   phone, social-worker reports and his final
>   email to his mother explaining his remorse.
>   It's quite eerie actually. It's almost as though
>   he knew he was going to die

ADE   (*aside*) there is so much I want to say…
>   But I don't.
>   I'm too frozen in an unexplainable emotion
>   that makes me want to run away.
>   But I can't.

ADE *exhales*.

>   Emily says she'll tell my agent that I'm
>   interested.
>   She swiftly hangs up the call
>   meeting is done, 'cause
>   she's offloaded the 'story' she's come to share.
>   A story that's just story for her
>   but a reality for people like me

Silence.

Scene Three

ADE   (*aside*) it all happened so fast
>   at a speed my brain couldn't race to catch

ADE*'s phone pings*.

>   A story of a black boy that I don't know, but I
>   instantly felt his pain. Like the story of many
>   young kids gone before their time.

ADE *touches her heart*.

>   I explain it all to my mum, whilst she sits in

	her kitchen and looks at me. Examines me You know what mums are like
MUM	You can't handle stories like this Ade. You're not like me and your sister. You're sensitive, you've always been. You don't read the newspapers, you can't watch the news. And heaven forbid I tell you what I hear on *Crimewatch*. Why are you doing this project?
ADE	I… I don't know if I am, Mum. I haven't decided yet. My agent says it's a greenlight, so she thinks I should consider it properly
MUM	Is that all you're worth? A greenlight?
ADE	Mum, I've never had my own show
MUM	Ade, you had '*Big Gal Tings*'
ADE	Mum, *Big Gal Tings* was a short – it was twenty-five minutes
MUM	welllllllll it got you a BAFTA nomination. That's a big deal.
ADE	I know it has. Did. And I'm happy. But this show, 'JJ's story' would be my first TV series with something that's more than one episode.
MUM	Adetola, why do you compromise yourself?
ADE	Mum, it's not compromise, it's me doing what I've gotta do to get by, and 'getting by' pays my bills, keeps me in London and the occasional yoga class…
	(*aside*) My mum looks at me with her knowing eyes and deep down, I know she's right.
	My agent says it's a greenlight. An opportunity to showcase my talent.

But what is my talent?

What does a man gain if he inherits the world but loses his soul?

The problem is what can I do?

Have you've ever done something you don't wonna do?

Compromised yourself?

Felt extra pressure to do it 'cause of your 'background'

Because you're a woman
                    you're black.

On many occasions I look around me and I see that I'm one of the few people in the room who feels this.

I watch my mum, and through the years she has attained so much strength.

Strength to be who she is, unapologetic.

And I'd love to be in that place
                  but I'm not
                        yet.

  Shit that was honest.

Mum neatly pulls the clothes out of the washing machine, and routinely folds them. Seeing her enjoy something so mundane makes me wish for that.
For a quietness that comes from being at peace with yourself.

MUM   Are you staying over tonight?

ADE   nah, I've gotta be back into London for Leanne's birthday party

	(*aside*) Mum sighs and rolls her eyes. I know what she's thinking. Mum + Leanne = bitch gone kill my vibe.
MUM	well if you need a lift to the station your sister will be back from school soon
ADE	I'm not having my seventeen-year-old sister drive me around the shires of Norwich, it's already bad enough that I can't drive. I can't be shown up by my baby sister
MUM	You could have driven but you preferred London transport. Now look where that's got you?
ADE	Yeah. A thirty-three-year-old, living on her own, in a flat in Vauxhall that has perfect connections to the city and plenty of Lime bikes to choose from. I'm living my ancestors' dream. (*aside*) Mum knows she can't argue with this, so she turns back to folding clothes, whilst I look up the next train to London. Even though I'm a Londoner through and through, I love having my mum's new 'work home' in Norwich to retire to. I think all of this, as I swiftly gather my things and walk the twenty minutes to the station. Eager to miss my baby sister flexing in her new wheels.

Sounds of the high street and train station merge with the music ADE *is listening to.*

ADE	On the train home, I reluctantly slot into the only inside seat left on the train.
	I literally and figuratively try not to take up any space.
	As usual. Whilst the man next to me uses this as a chance to spread into mine.

I rest my jacket between us, and his elbow
still pokes through and jabs into my side
                              my ribs
whilst he reads his not *so* broadsheet.
I try to ignore him… there's only ninety
minutes left till London.
I open my emails see the subject matter 'JJ's
story'…
       I open it
Hover over his first of twenty-five voices
notes
He was only twelve…

ADE*'s phone pings with a new email.*

An email pops in from Jessica labelled
URGENT…
In caps
Caps is never good
I open it
Scroooolllll down and see that 'the casting
announcement for *Day Girl* has been met with
some challenging opinions'
but I shouldn't worry 'cause 'the theatre is
preparing a press statement'
Press statement
Is it really that serious?!

I open Twitter and the comments flood me

Comments flood in as voice-overs.

COMMENT 1   aren't we tired of rich instagrammers taking opportunities from real actors

COMMENT 2   Denise is fake

COMMENT 3   worked the 'working class' to get her Henley arse to the top

COMMENT 4   The creative team behind this show should be ashamed.

COMMENT 5 This is sickening!

COMMENT 6 Denise is a spoilt rich kid, why are you giving her this platform?

COMMENT 7 Fraud

COMMENT 8 why would you cast her when you know she's a rich nepo baby. This is poor taste. Think about all the real actors who could of had this job.

COMMENT 9 Boycott this show! It's bullshit

COMMENT 10 why is she talking like that? That's not even her real accent. This is Yuck!

Cacophony of sound.

ADE (*aside*)
Their comments follow me home
                      they shower with me

Sounds of the comments play in the background.

I didn't know Denise was a…
                Isn't really a
                    Am I to blame too?

I get dressed
        throw on anything.

I can't think past the thoughts in my head.

Sounds of the comments distort then morph into the bass of a nightclub track.

Scene Four

The bass in the club is overbearingly loud.

ADE I'm in the club
and I can barely hear Leanne
Leanne is my cousin, aunt…
My aunt who's a year younger than me
and went to the same primary school as me.
So it was easier to call her my cousin even
though she's technically my aunt…
My grandad's youngest daughter, my dad's
baby sister who is younger than his actual
daughter… Me.

Leanne looks me dead in eyes and tries to
fight against the noise from the speakers…

LEANNE yooo, cussy wa gwan with the writing tings?
I've been seeing what they're saying on
socials about *Day Girl*. Mad. It's like you've
fallen off. You went from acting in your own
fings. To now you're just a writer. Are you
even still an actor? You did '*Big Girl Tings*' in
Edinburgh… then what?

ADE (*aside*) she knows what? She was there
for the what… the London transfer, New
York remount, TV version and BAFTA
nomination… She knows 'what' was but she's
not talking about that she's *really* talking
about

LEANNE *inhales from her vape.*

LEANNE I feel like you sold out, man. Like on a real
you hired people who ain't us to play us. Now
look. Why you always giving our shit away to
them when we're right here. I can act… I did
Sylvia Young as a kid. Ain't you supposed to
be flexing some nepotism and shit?

	LEANNE *inhales from her vape and blows her smoke around.*
	It's crazy man. I was even talking to my mum about it... getting her perspective on fings
ADE	(*aside*) Leanne's mum Claudette has never liked me... I don't know why. When my grandad remarried and blended our Nigerian home into an actual Afro-Caribbean soirée, I thought our only war would be between 'plantin'' and 'plantain'.
	Why did you talk to your mum, Leanne? You could have come to me
LEANNE	What can I say... Mumsy saw I was down and that... and I couldn't lie... ya know... Money's low and I could have done with some help
	ADE *nods. She's drifting... she knows where it's going.*
LEANNE	It would have been good, cus. Get a little bit of support and whatnot. But I get it... you're West End status now... We're just ends init
ADE	(*aside*) Leanne has never thought I was 'ends' enough. Even though my estate was only two streets away from hers. She saw the difference between her SW9 and my SW8 as worlds apart.
	My mum bought our council flat in the nineties, much like the other people in our block who worked hard and finally owned something of their own. A dream that their parents had wished for when they immigrated to this country, under pretence of roads paved in gold. But when they arrived they were met with

No Dogs
No Blacks
No Irish

They still worked hard
Made this place a home
And unlike some of our neighbours, my mum never sold our flat for a 'quieter life' in the country.
She left it as a place for me to live.
She knew I'd never leave London.
It's my home

So I never get why Leanne or other people see me as not 'being ends enough', when the same South London streets raised me.

LEANNE *inhales from her vape and blows her smoke around.*

Leanne inhales from her vape as the blue mist wraps around us, in this nightclub that is full way beyond its capacity.
                Kinda like me.

Leanne beckons a waiter over, scans the menu orders a double then gestures for the waiter to present the card machine to me.

ADE *taps her card.*

Like many times, I should say something
                              but I don't.

ADE *sighs.*

Three hours later and my wallet's feeling emptier, I arrive back in my area, with Leanne's words circling in my mind

LEANNE   (*voice-over*) We're just ends init…

ADE   They follow me down my street

LEANNE	(*voice-over*) just ends init…
ADE	as I look for my keys
LEANNE	(*voice-over*) end it…

ADE's phone pings with an email notification, whilst Leanne's words circle in her mind.

ADE My phone beeps, and I see another work email pour in above the email marked 'JJ's story'.

He was just twelve.

ADE *calls* TOBI.

I know its 2 a.m. but Tobi's my best friend I can call him anytime

It goes to voicemail.

TOBI (*on voicemail*) You've reached the voicemail for Tobi Oludeji. You know what to do.

ADE This is so annoying. I wish you could pick up your phone. I wish….

ADE's *voicemail message continues.*

(*on voicemail*) I have soooo much to tell you. I need my best friend. I wish you could call me back please? Or we could go to an open mic in Soho… or you could just come over. I need cuddles with my bestie, and just real talk. Like fuck. I feel like no one's getting me lately. And you always make me feel less weird. Less out of this world… Fuck… Fuck – This sounds emo. I just need to hear your voice. I miss you. I love

ADE *sighs and ends the call.*

STRANGER (*voice-over*) ADE… ADEE!

ADE In the distance I can hear shouting
I can hear my name.
It can't be my name

	not this late
	I ignore it and continue to my block
	But the voice gets louder.
STRANGER	(*voice-over*) ADE... ADEE!
ADE	I turn around and a
	White noise.
	a slap lands across my face
	I look up and I see a woman.
	A woman I don't know
	but she seems to know who I am.
STRANGER	(*voice-over*) You gave me chlamydia, you fucking slut. You nasty bitch. I've been working overseas making money for my family and you're fucking my husband. We have kids ya know.
ADE	husband... kids? (*aside*) I tell her that I don't know her husband.
	Then she shows me pictures.
	Our pictures.
	Me and Marcus's pictures.
	My naked body on his phone.
	Our moments that I thought were real
STRANGER	(*voice-over*) You're lucky revenge porn is a crime.
ADE	I throw up.
	She recoils and kisses her teeth, spits at me, then she runs away
	I wonna do something
	anything
	but what if she knows where I work?
	where my mum lives
	where I
	I
	I should do something
	anything

but what if its my fault?
did I know?
did I?

I replay our interactions, the times when Marcus would stay and his recent excuses to leave

The thoughts circle my brain, whilst I search for clues and head to my flat.

Lie on my bed
Turn to my phone.
I should block him
    I need to block him
        I will
            but I don't
                not yet.

He might call
    might apologise
        tell me its not true.

I change his name from Marcus to
    'Do Not Answer'

ADE *sighs and is restless.*

2.30 a.m. and I can't sleep
    My heads ringing
    My face is sore
    Is she gonna come back?
    I keep replaying
    Thinking did I know?
    I need to speak to Marcus
        no, Tobi
    Somebody
    Anybody who understands

I need to channel my mind into something else.

    Work
    'I've got a lot on'
    Stories

>   Half finished
>   I should complete them
>   JJ's
>   JJ's 'story'
>   Should I
>   It's a greenlight

> It's an opportunity for someone like me
>   I should try and sleep
>   But I can't.

>   Should I open JJ's story?

Suspenseful sounds build.

Scene Five

ADE The next day I arrive at the theatre, after
barely any sleep.
My mind is full of thoughts of JJ.
His 'story'.
His voicenotes
His final email
It rests on my shoulders, as I uncomfortably
sit in the auditorium of the theatre for what
is meant to be 'stage practice', but the only
person practising is me…
I'm working on trying to put aside everything
that happened last night
what I read in JJ's research file
the trolls comments about Denise and *Day Girl*
the ideas I need to write
the pitches I need to perfect
and the meetings I need to prep for.
The workload that keeps on loading
                    loading and
                              loading

like my new Hinge profile.
According to Google, the best way to get over someone is to meet someone new...
But who knew online dating would be this bleak
Between filtering out the uncles
the humans who might actually be AI
and conversations based just on emojis

I'm left with 0 matches...

All of these thoughts
Work...
    Life...
      Unbalanced
Wrestle in my mind till I settle on one

Where is everyone?

I check the schedule

'10.30 a.m. – stage time Denise and Susie'

I'm the only one here.
I call Jessica, the producer

ADE *is diverted to voicemail*.

She diverts my call to voicemail.

I ring back again

ADE *is diverted to voicemail again. Her phone pings*.

Then she texts me to say 'come up to the office'

I've never been to the office.
                        This must be serious.

I take the lift up to the fourth floor and I'm greeted by floor-to-ceiling rows of plays

Texts dating this theatre from its 1890s origin to now.
Jessica appears, then ushers me over to the sofas, whilst she heads to the kitchen.
I nestle into the sofa and almost fall asleep when she reappears.
She places a cup of tea and biscuits in front of me
it's meant to be comforting
        but it's not.
It's tense
  but I don't know why…

There's something she wants to say but the words haven't found a way to escape, yet.
Usually she'd turn to Lu for reassurance, but she's on annual leave taking in the Mediterranean breeze.
Whilst Jessica has to find the right words to say

JESSICA   We've never experienced this before. I'm flabbergasted. It's *not* slay. We're having to consult a PR agency to help us to reword our statement.

ADE   is… is that why rehearsals aren't happening in the theatre today?

JESSICA   Susie and Denise have taken a self-care day. They need some time to process it all. Which gives you more time to work on some edits and make the show more…

ADE   (*aside*) She stops mid-sentence. As if the media training that she's been waiting to receive has advised her to say less.
There is so much I want to say, but I don't know how.
I stare into my tea and the thought of *Get Out* sends shudders down my spine.

I instinctively say my thank-yous
> nod diligently
> and leave.

I stand outside of the theatre.
Stare at the poster with Denise's face and my
name underneath, lined up next to posters
with faces that look like hers and names that
don't sound like mine.

I head home and work on *Day Girl* edits
I type then re-type
I type and then delete
I sit
Eat
Don't masturbate
Google
Search
Is writer's block even real?
> 'apparently not'

what do you do when you're stuck? Where do
you turn to?

He looks at me and doesn't say anything
> or maybe

he says something but I'm not listening
I'm too busy judging myself for letting him in
There is a reason why I labelled him 'do not
answer' but yet here he is, sitting on the end
of my bed like nothing ever happened…
> but it did…

We spoke it about it
> a bit
> > but not properly
> > > not fully

> I should ask him..
> > I'm gonna ask him

Marcus, why didn't you tell me you're
married?

TING	Like I said before, Ade. It's complicated yeah. She thinks we're still together but we ain't. We ain't been together for time
ADE	If you ain't been with her, then who you been with?
	(*aside*) I think we're having our first argument which goes against the rules of a 'situationship'. You never ask the other person who they've been with that is a no-go conversation... but if his wife is correct and they're still together then this isn't a situationship... I am a certified side chick And as a side chick I deserve answers
TING	Babes why you asking me something like that? We don't talk about dem tings there.
ADE	(*aside*) Oh he's guilty he is so guilty. Okay, if you don't wonna talk about that Marcus, then tell me why your wife thinks I gave you chlamydia?
TING	She said that? That's wild. I don't even know why she'd say that
ADE	Marcus when was the last time you got tested?
TING	I dunno. I'm not out here spreading my seed everywhere... I don't need to get tested like that... I think the last time I got tested was like nine... ten year ago.
ADE	(*aside*) nine ten What?! Marcus can tell the atmosphere in the room

has changed
It's gotten serious.
He doesn't like it.
He asks me if I want him to stay over
I say no, I've got a lot to do.
He turns away from me, like so many times
before, pulls his clothes on and leaves... but
this time I don't feel alone...

    I weirdly feel relieved.
I wonna tell Tobi, 'cause I know he'll be
proud of me... but I'll update him later.

I jump on a Lime bike
    head to Soho
        dock the bike
            and walk
                no run
                    run...
                        to the clinic

this is important

I check in
And wait
And wait

NURSE   (*voice-over*) – Serena Minaj

ADE   Serena Minaj is the alias I created when I was
fifteen just in case someone my mum knows
catches me in here
Nigerian mum's + sex before marriage = it's
not worth the wahala.

I sit in the uncomfortable chair
Explain to the nurse about my situation
She tests me
Screens me for everything and I do mean
everything...
Even though I always use condoms but you
never know about the stuff that spills over the
edges or the back of your throat or sometimes

in your eye.

When I leave the clinic Soho is in her full
glory and I love her for that.
I journey through Dean Street

ADE *stops and smiles. She hears singing.*

And the nostalgia takes over. I stand in front
of Kiki's bar
Tobi's favourite open-mic spot
Which then became mine…
You know the bestie effect
What's his is mine
              and what's mine is mine…
I should really call him

ADE *takes out her phone to call Tobi, but her
phone pings with a text message.*

Then my phone pings with an urgent message
from Jessica…
I'm needed at the theatre.

I contemplate whether I should go
              I know I should
                    must

I head to the theatre…

Inside the auditorium Jessica and the new
PR agent, who's giving off major Miranda
Priestly from *Devil Wears Prada* energy, are
waiting for me.
There are minimal hellos, no small talk.
This must be serious.
They tell me they have prepared a press
statement.
It's scheduled to go live in fifteen minutes.
They gesture a piece of paper in front of me
I read it.
I cry.

> I can't stop crying.
> I try to hide it.
> Jessica says with the support of the PR agent:

JESSICA We can see you're very emotional about this. If you're not able to handle this we can discuss it with your agent.

ADE No

> (*aside*) I respond.
> Still trying to wrap my head around the statement that shares that the show is being cancelled, for reasons beyond their control.
> Cancelled.
> Finished.
> Denise no longer wants to do this show
> neither does Susie
> so they can't.
> There's no time to re-rehearse
> To go over the dream.
> My dream
> A dream that I had, that was meant to become a reality has now been pushed to the side like so many before. It rests on my shoulders. As I leave the theatre.
> Get on the train to Norwich and I sift…
> I sift through the comments below the press statement on the theatres Twitter, and the once negative thoughts have shifted to my DMs…
> strangers apologising that this happened to me…
> that they had bought tickets…
> that seeing my name on an off-West End stage gave them hope to aim for that…
> I read message
> after message as I stand on the two-hour train to Norwich…
> I wanted to sit, but the thought of literally

have to shrink myself into a seat doesn't make me feel good today...
I stand instead
Trying to find my strength and for some reason I'm drawn to watch the thing that brought me to this point...
The story of being a big gal, a plus-size queen living in South London

(*voice-over*) Now don't get it twisted, I'm a big gal. I got all of this body... but please tell me why I ain't got an arse. Like no lie. It's okay, you can laugh – I've made peace with it. A guy I was once smashing was tapping my arse in bed, and I was like 'babe that's my back'... I literally have long back. Like what the actual fuck?! Like God... Why you gotta do me like that. Sir Mix-a-Lot talked about liking big butts, and I feel a lot of pressure ya know. My people have a reputation of having big gnashes... well I guess God was like 'sis your boobs sit fine, be happy with that sha'... yeah in my mind God is Nigerian. I'll be so disappointed if she isn't, 'cause the way she dishes out small small blessings she really be moving like a Nigerian auntie who is like 'you can't have it all now, you need to take your time o'

I watch my entire performance on the train to Norwich and I don't know about you but I usually hate seeing myself on camera...
But it feels good to see myself

In the background the train conductor announces: 'Ladies and gentlemen we are reaching our final stop, Norwich, please take all of your belongings with you.'

I leave the station. And I spot my baby sister,

looking like a parent eagerly waiting for her child

My sister spots me, beeps her horn and can't resist the temptation to say 'get in loser'.

She speeds down the country lane, way too fast for my liking but what do I know 'I cant drive'...

When we arrive at their home. My mum's sitting in the living room at her laptop on a video call to my dad.
    This can't be good.
I turn to look at my sister but she's already disappeared.
My mum beckons me into the room
                I really don't want to
but years of experience of being her daughter has taught me there is no point running.
My mum surveys my outfit
                my hoodie that I might have been wearing for a bit longer than I should of...
I feel like I'm being judged, especially when she turns to the camera and speaks to my dad

MUM   See this is what I was talking about Samuel. She's unkempt. This is why I need your help

ADE   (*aside*) For my mum to actually vocalise that she needs help, it must be bad...
                I must be

ADE *sniffs her armpit... it smells bad.*

Dad leans closer to the camera, whilst Lagos lives on behind him and it's like he peers into my soul. My dad and I weren't close growing up, especially when my parents broke up. But when I became an adult
                so did he.
He admitted to being too young to be a parent

| | and I admitted I was tired of being disappointed in him.
So that made our bond grow tighter
stronger.
Which is why he can be here on a video call with me and my mum.
Dad looks at Mum and nods.
Then says something that I don't think I register… |
|---|---|
| **DAD** | Ade, your mum and I want you to go to therapy |
| **ADE** | Wait what?
My parents are suggesting that *I* need to go to therapy…
before them.
I'm sorry but are my issues that bad?
So bad that they haven't suggested that I pray about it?!
'Cause my people believe in the power of prayer not in telling a stranger our business.
We're secretive
we don't chat each other's business
that's called snitching
maybe Leanne's right, I'm not ends.
My mum picks up where my dad has tailed off |
| **MUM** | Ade. We're worried about you and how you're coping. It would be good for you to talk to someone outside of us about how you're dealing with work and grieving Tobi. His mum told me you're still calling his phone. |
| | *Silence.* |
| **ADE** | My mum slips a paper in my hand and it's a self-referral form.
My parents keep talking to me, and I can't stop staring at the questions…
the words on the page that refer to me… and |

| | deep down I know they are right.
I spend the next two days, cooped up at my mum's trying to get my head away from everything.
We watch movies, *The Real Housewives* and my mum blasts Elton John's 'I'm Still Standing'... She tells me:

MUM this should be your new anthem. Your motivational song whilst you're getting back on your feet

ADE (*aside*) I hate to break it to her but as much as I know Elton John is a living legend, his music style isn't really my vibe... I'm more emo mixed with a lot of Drake... but I get where she's going with it.

'I'm Still Standing' plays.

regardless, I sit there and listen to her and Elton playing in the living room and I see why she's suggested this song.
This sign of triumph...
To keep...
   keep going...
      oh shit!
      I have to go.
I clock the time and realise I need to go back to London for a press night that I'm due to attend.
I can't not go
Not after everything.
I don't want people to think I've fallen off or that I'm...

Mum looks at me and I can see what she's thinking.
I take her hand into mine and reassure her
'I'm still standing'...
I say it with a conviction

a conviction that I'm not sure that I have yet.
But I have to go.
Now.
You know my whole thing about being late.

Sounds of the high street and train station merge with the music ADE *is listening to.*

Scene Six

The only sound in the train carriage is from ADE*'s headphones.*

ADE	On the train back to London I find a rare empty seat. For the first time in ages, I get to sit alone Well I'm not alone fully 'Cause I've checked my emails and see an URGENT one from Jessica
JESSICA	(*voice-over*) The press want a follow-up. We have an urgent meeting at the theatre tonight
ADE	Then an email from my agent
LOTTIE	(*voice-over*) any word on your take for JJ's story? Emily wants to schedule a pitch meeting tomorrow?
ADE	Then a text from my aunt/cousin Leanne
LEANNE	(*voice-over*) mad tings about your play cus. Just seen everything online… Boy you must be depressed.
ADE	I put my phone on do not disturb for the next two hours then I look out of the window and enjoy the silence for once.

3.30 p.m.
I arrive back in London
                Liverpool Street.

I know I was meant to hit that press night, but
I keep replaying the look my mum gave me...
a look that says 'is that all you're worth'...
and she's right... I'm worth more.
So I walk in the direction of a place I haven't
visited in a while...

Sound of church bells.

I stand
    unsure of whether to sit or
                            stand

ADE *looks down.*

I decide it's best to kneel

I look down at Tobi...
The stone that marks his begin till when I
found him
   with a note
The time when he officially left but I still hold
pieces of him
       here

ADE *indicates to heart.*

Tobi
I think I've found new a phrase 'Le therapy
experience'... I'm not sure it has a ring to it
yet... But I'm trying it out.
My parents want me to go to le therapy
I know
I can't believe it before them
It's crazy
But maybe its time...

(*aside*) I feel tears forming in my eyes so I
look away
   he never liked it when I cried

ADE *exhales*.

I take a moment then I tell him everything
Things that I wonna keep between us
But I'll summarise.

I tell him I feel like a failure.
Like everything I wanted.
Dreamed of.
Has come crashing around me.
And the closer I got
                get to 'achieving it'
                        or whatever 'it' is...
Actually I know what the fuck 'it' is.
It's the dream that every person who has ever
felt overlooked pins on your back and weighs
on your shoulders because you want to do
well for not just you but for them. Them who
are constantly erased from history, who are
'shown support' but without actually being
given support.
Who have to keep going even though they
want to stop
    'cause when you win, we all win so you
have to keep 'winning'
even if you feel like you're losing
                        losing yourself
and everything that got you to this point brings
you further away from the person you once
were but you assure
        reassure yourself that one day you
will say something but that one day doesn't
always come
so it just sits inside of you
                    and you agree
                    you just nod
                    you get by to get by
but it's exhausting
It's tiring

I don't want to have to keep doing it any more...
I am tired.

And I hate myself for being this fucking vulnerable
Vulnerability fucking sucks
Urgggghhh

Fuck it

ADE *speaks to Tobi*.

I miss you Tobi
I really fucking do
I hate the fact that you left me here without you
I hate it
But I understand
No I don't fucking understand b
But maybe one day I will
                    I will

ADE *exhales*.

Something about saying all of this makes me feel exhausted.
I wonna sit
    lay here
        next to him all night and talk to him some more
        but I can feel the caretaker looking at me
unsure of whether to approach...
Trying his best to be polite but I don't want to make him feel uncomfortable

So I gather what's left of me.

I refuse to say goodbye
                to him
                      to Tobi

    I'm not ready to let go yet.

6.30 p.m.

I stand outside of the theatre and the
CANCELLED sign stretches across
my show
my dream
my vision
and I feel so many conflicting things

ADE*'s phone pings.*

My feelings about *Day Girl* are overrun by
feelings of happiness to know that your girl
aka me… ain't got chlamydia or any STI…
Which makes me think I'm clearly not
Marcus's only situationship.
I finally do the right thing and block his
number…
     okay why am I lying to you. I archive
him.

I step.
    step into the theatre, trace down the
crimson corridor
into the auditorium where Jessica, Lu and the
PR agent are waiting for me.
It feels weird to be back in this place
                           this space that in
a week's time should've debuted my show.
Now the only thing it houses is my shame
                        my regret
                        my

I look at them and there is so much I want to
say
I don't
    I can't
        I must
            I've got to

ADE *takes a step forward.*

I'm Ade Adeyomi and you won't take away my voice or my dreams

ADE *exhales.*

Lights out.

End.

In the original Edinburgh production, at the end of the show, the audience were invited to take a rose from the stage and give it to a performer, artist, creative or anyone they feel needed a rose to symbolise they are seen and cared for.

A Nick Hern Book

failure project first published in Great Britain as a paperback original in 2024 by Nick Hern Books Limited, The Glasshouse, 49a Goldhawk Road, London, W12 8QP

failure project copyright © 2024 Yolanda Mercy

Yolanda Mercy has asserted her right to be identified as the author of this work

Cover design by Yolanda Mercy, photography of Yolanda Mercy by Richard Haynes

Designed and typeset by Nick Hern Books, London
Printed in Great Britain by Mimeo Ltd, Huntingdon, Cambridgeshire PE29 6XX

A CIP catalogue record for this book is available from the British Library

ISBN 978 1 83904 384 0

CAUTION All rights whatsoever in this play are strictly reserved. Requests to reproduce the text in whole or in part should be addressed to the publisher.

Amateur Performing Rights Applications for performance, including readings and excerpts, by amateurs in the English language should be addressed to the Performing Rights Manager, Nick Hern Books, The Glasshouse, 49a Goldhawk Road, London W12 8QP, *tel* +44 (0)20 8749 4953, *email* rights@nickhernbooks.co.uk, except as follows:

Australia: ORiGiN Theatrical, *tel* +61 (2) 8514 5201, *email* enquiries@originmusic.com.au, *web* www.origintheatrical.com.au

New Zealand: Play Bureau, 20 Rua Street, Mangapapa, Gisborne 4010, *tel* +64 21 258 3998, *email* info@playbureau.com

Professional Performing Rights Rights Applications for performance by professionals in any medium and in any language throughout the world should be addressed in the first instance to Nick Hern Books, see contact details above.

No performance of any kind may be given unless a licence has been obtained. Applications should be made before rehearsals begin. Publication of this play does not necessarily indicate its availability for amateur performance.

www.nickhernbooks.co.uk/environmental-policy

www.nickhernbooks.co.uk

facebook.com/nickhernbooks

twitter.com/nickhernbooks